Listening for God

Spiritual Directives
for
Searching Christians

Ben Campbell Johnson

PAULIST PRESS
New York / Mahwah, N.J.

Cover design by Jim Brisson

Library of Congress Cataloging-in-Publication Data

Johnson, Ben Campbell.
    Listening for God : spiritual directives for searching Christians / Ben Campbell Johnson.
        p.   cm.
    ISBN 0-8091-3718-6
    1. Spiritual exercises. I. Title.
BV4832.2.J
248.3—dc21   97-22781
                                                      CIP

Published by Paulist Press
997 Macarthur Boulevard
Mahwah, New Jersey 07430

Printed and bound in the
United States of America

CONTENTS

INTRODUCTION

These Spiritual Directives aim to guide you in finding and doing the will of God in your life. The audience for whom these suggestions were written is rather broad: for beginners who do not know where they are on the journey, for mature persons who have reached a crisis point and need to refocus their lives, and for persons who have grown weary in their obedience and seek renewal of faith and love. The directives do not magically help you find your way, but they do focus on crucial passages of scripture that invite you into a variety of discernment experiences. The suggestions are intended to help create an environment in which you may encounter the Spirit and hear God's call more clearly.

The idea for these directives was inspired by the Spiritual Exercises of St. Ignatius, who, more than four hundred years ago, wrote "exercises" to be used in discerning a call to the religious life. By contrast, these directives have a broader audience and purpose—written primarily to help persons move with greater freedom and purpose in their faith journeys wherever they may begin.

While the method has been borrowed from St. Ignatius, both the structure and process in these directives are my own. The various approaches to the scriptures have grown out of my personal experiences of listening for God. From time to time I have encountered God through these different avenues into the text. Not only have these approaches been helpful to me, but many other persons who have used them testify to their benefit. I trust that you also will find these directives helpful in your search.

On Using the Directives

The thirty directives may be used over thirty consecutive days (though most will take more than one day to complete), or they may be used as a guide for a three- or five-day retreat. If you use them for a retreat, one section may prove more helpful than another and you should not feel compelled to attempt all thirty exercises over a short period of time. The directives fall into three sections: Preparation for God's Call (1–7); Listening for God's Call in Christ (8–24); and Finding Support for the Call in Community (25–30).

Begin these directives with a spirit of expectancy. You have a desire to know the purpose of your life; *God wills that you find meaning and direction for living out your days.* These directives invite you into a variety of experiences that will help you satisfy your hunger through an encounter with God and God's intention for you.

You will be more likely to succeed in your meeting with God if you set a time and a place daily to read, reflect, and pray. Make this the most important appointment of your day. Don't let anything cause you to neglect it. Should you fail in your resolve, don't become overly burdened with guilt. Simply begin again where you left off.

The Structure of the Directives

Each directive begins with an affirmation of faith, moving from the faith statement to an appropriation of the truth of that statement. This personalizing of the faith occurs through a psalm, a personal prayer for guidance, and reflections on a scripture text. The Guide to the text offers several suggestions for approaching the scripture to be considered. The concluding prayer offers help in formulating your heart's desire.

Neither the opening nor the closing prayer seeks to manipulate your desires or to inhibit your free expression; they are not exhaustive but are intentionally sketchy, leaving room for your inspiration. Give free rein to your imagination and write prayers drawing on the images, ideas, and longings that grow out of your encounter with God.

Do not permit these suggestions to become confining or oppressive; let them direct, suggest, and point but *when your imagination becomes enlivened by a text, prayer, or thought, stay with your inspiration rather than rigidly following the directives.* (Treat the exercise as an invitation to an adventure, not a class assignment to be completed! Give attention to the ideas that attract you without any compulsion to complete the suggestions.)

Some persons have requested shorter, simpler directions for getting into the text. Others have experienced difficulty in using their imagination; writing has been problematic for another group. In response to several requests, I have prepared an alternative set of directives, each of which is listed following the Guide to the text.

The Alternative guide to the text may be used instead of the suggestions under Guide to the text or at a later time as a way of reviewing your discernment process. These alternative directives are not "easier" but seek to employ a slightly different approach for sensate, thinking personalities. Some of them call for crayons, clay, large pieces of paper, and so forth. If you choose the alternative directives, plan ahead to ensure you have the required materials.

How to Proceed with a Directive

I have adopted this particular structure for the directives because each movement builds on the previous one. Begin the time of reflection by entering the place you have consecrated for prayer. Spend a few minutes preparing yourself for meditation.

Read the introductory statement. Pause and reflect on the content of the faith statements.

Pray the psalm selection. Think about each of the words, and permit these thoughts to lead you into a deeper awareness of God. Pray the invocation (the first prayer) printed in the directive, pause—let the Spirit take you more deeply into your heart and the latent prayer waiting to be offered. Spend several minutes centering your attention and waiting before the Lord.

Read the scripture text. Read slowly, letting each word speak to you. Underline words and phrases that grasp you, speak to you, or interest you. Be present to the truth of the text. Free your imagination to freely associate your life with the ideas in the text.

Follow the suggestions. Permit them to guide you into the text. *If an inspiration comes to you, stay with it and do not feel compelled to mechanically finish all the suggestions that remain in this section.*

Write your thoughts and inspirations. Writing your responses to the text is very important. Material from your deeper self surfaces more readily when you write your thoughts than when you simply think about the text. I offer these suggestions to you for only one reason—to help you look at the text until it speaks to your life situation.

Pray. Make your own prayer when you have completed the directive. Allow the printed prayer to suggest content for your own prayer. When you finish the directive, wait in silence for the Lord to speak to you. Reflect on the ideas, feelings, and inspirations that have come to you in the exercise.

Following this order will help you derive the most benefit from each of these directives.

Explaining Spiritual Practices

As you engage the directives you will find suggestions like "prepare for meditation," "meditate on," "contemplate the text," "write a dialogue," or "journal." Since these terms may be unfamiliar to you, I will give you clear explanations and directions for each of these practices.

Preparation for Meditation. Preparation may be as important as the meditation itself. Always take a few minutes to prepare. Get both your mind and your body set. Relax and focus your attention. Preparation often makes the difference between a fulfilling and a frustrating time of meditation.

In planning your meditation, set a time and designate a place. Many persons find that engaging in meditation about the same time and in the same place helps both concentration and consistency. Choose the time of day when you are most alert and least likely to be interrupted.

Decide on a place. The place should be free of noise or other disturbances. It should be comfortable physically and have adequate light. Using the same place daily tends to consecrate that place so that you get accustomed to meeting God there. Going into that space is itself an act of preparation.

Sit erect and make room for your breath. Choose a posture that helps you to ignore your body.

Relax. It is hard for us to open ourselves deeply to God with a tense, strained body. A few techniques will help. Take eight or ten deep breaths. Breathe slowly, concentrating on the air entering your body and being expelled from it. Think of breathing in peace and breathing out tension. Continue this exercise until you feel relaxed.

Two other exercises may be helpful: count your breaths. With your attention on your breathing, count your first breath in as one, your first breath out as two, and so on up to ten. At ten begin with one again. Continue this until your mind is clear and your body relaxed.

Or, you may seek to drain the tension out of your body. Picture the tension in your head, behind your eyes (wherever you feel tight), draining through your neck, shoulders, down your arms, and dripping out of your body through the tips of your fingers. Continue draining out the tension until you are relaxed.

A Way to Meditate. Since meditation may be an experience you are just beginning, I will explain one way to engage in it creatively. Meditation involves a deliberate, disciplined act of focusing your attention on a word, phrase, or other subject until it speaks to you. For example, in the First Directive I suggest that you meditate on the goodness of creation. Here are ways to proceed once you have prepared yourself according to the guidelines I have suggested above.

Think: "Creation is good." Repeat the phrase several times slowly. Begin to ask yourself questions about this statement. What does it mean to say "Creation is good"? How is creation good? What is there in creation that contradicts this assertion? What does the goodness of creation mean to my evaluation of myself? How does the goodness of creation affect my sense of place and task in life?

Any one of these questions may engage your attention for the whole period of your meditation. Do not surrender to the compulsion to rush an answer to all of these questions. Try to find one or two questions that engage you and stay with them.

If your mind wanders, gently bring it back. Keep at the task. If a question leads you down a fruitful path, follow it.

The practice of meditation is different from an intellectual inquiry or an analysis. In an inquiry into the "goodness of creation" your goal might be to construct a logical argument to convince a skeptic or to comfort a sufferer. In meditation you aim to open yourself to this truth so that it may penetrate the deepest levels of your psyche. Insight into truth provides the medium of your communion with God. Meeting God is your aim in meditation, not gathering data.

These two approaches to truth require contrasting mental postures: the one active, the other receptive. An active mind aggressively pursues facts in order to know. A receptive mind waits relaxed and open to receive the divine presence and to commune with God. Both movements of human knowing have an important place; meditation aims at convictional knowing while discursive thought aims at rational understanding.

Contemplating Scripture. I believe the knowledge of God and the validation of God's will must be sought in the text of scripture and offer you guidance in one way to engage the text—the Ignatian method.

After reading the text, close your eyes and review the major elements in the encounter with Jesus in these specific ways: Imagine that you are actually present, viewing the event; notice all the details of the setting, such as the other persons present, the physical environment, the weather, and other objects that might be in the scene.

Use your sense of smell. What odors or aromas can you smell? Is the air in your nose dry or moist?

Listen for sounds. Be aware of all the sounds that are occurring in this scene in Jesus' life. What do other people say? What animals can you hear? What are the sounds of nature—thunder, the blowing wind, the pounding rain? Listen to your own breathing.

What tastes do you experience? Does the air taste dry? What other tastes might you have in this particular setting?

Having noted in detail the setting for the encounter, become the person to whom Jesus ministers or (in the case of his passion) enter into the feelings of Christ. As you identify with the person in the narrative, write the story in first-person language as though you are reporting the experience to a friend. Give your imagination free reign as you write. Ideas will come to you that you have never had before.

Writing may seem difficult or nonessential at the beginning. Write anyway and you will engage Christ in much greater depth than if you merely recounted the episode in your mind.

Read your report. Listen for Christ's word to you in the narrative. Give careful consideration to Christ's call as you listen receptively to the Spirit.

Search your heart after this encounter. What do you desire from Christ? Ask him for your deepest desires whether or not this is included in the Guide to the text. Wait before him for his answer.

Writing a Dialogue. Often I invite you to write a dialogue with Christ or with God. In writing a dialogue you must supply both sides of the conversation through your own mind. For example, to write a dialogue with Christ, pose a question to him. It may involve a concern that the text has awakened in you or it may have another source. Write the question.

Be silent and listen to the response that comes to you. Write it down. Ponder this response for a few minutes and then shift your concern to writing a response to what Christ says. Continue the process of questioning, listening, and responding until nothing else comes to you.

After pondering the last response Christ makes, review the completed dialogue. What do you learn about his will for you? About yourself? The review may inspire further dialogue. If so, continue to write.

This procedure may raise fears of delusion in you. Am I not projecting my own unconscious desires into the mouth of Christ and am I not getting divine confirmation of my own desires?

Of course, this self-deception is always possible. To avoid gross self-delusion take the answer with an openness to be corrected. Do not rule out the possibility that Christ does speak to you through your own intuition and imagination. Test the answers that come to you. No word from Christ will contradict his Spirit and teaching in the scriptures. If you have a question about the authenticity of his word to you, talk about it with a Spiritual Friend.

Just a word about writing. While the dialogue can occur as a mental exercise, ideas flow more freely when you write. If you do not write, you lose the record for review and future reference.

This approach to listening to Christ has been effective for many serious seekers of God's will. Your own discoveries will be the best evidence of its value as a devotional tool.

On Journaling. The invitation to keep a journal places you in a long line of Christ's followers who have found this a helpful discipline. A *journal* as we use the term is a record of your interaction with God. In a larger sense the journal will include everything going on in your spiritual journey, but the journal in this exercise will be used specifically to record both your answers to questions and the experiences you have in response to specific directives.

Each text in the particular directive is followed by a series of suggestions called Guide to the text. These suggestions indicate different ways to appropriate the truth of the scripture into our quest for God's will for our lives.

Most suggestions require writing. Even when you can do the exercise in your mind, write your answers so that you will have a record for future reference. Those suggestions that invite you to reflect on or ponder an idea will produce thoughts and feelings to record. Keep a record of these experiences. When you have completed the thirty directives you will be glad that you kept a log of the journey.

Writing in the journal has numerous benefits. First, writing permits the free flow of ideas, often eliciting knowledge that you did not know you possessed. Writing permits review and evaluation. After a period of time elapses, the written record becomes a source of encouragement as the promises of God are verified or as struggles finally end. You will also discover that some of the things Christ said to you in the written dialogues were indeed his word for you.

Embark on the journal experience with expectation.

When you encounter these terms in the directives, review their meaning and how best to practice these particular exercises.

Examine Your Consciousness Daily

At the end of each day reflect on what has taken place in your life. This discipline is called "an examination of consciousness." Recall your thoughts, feelings, inspirations, the persons you met, and moments when you may have failed in your high intentions. Make a few notes in your journal chronicling your experience of the day. This daily examination will help keep you focused and will deepen your consciousness of our Lord's work in your life.

John Carroll Futrell offers a simple way to gather the day and offer it to God. He suggests four short prayers that cover the crucial issues:

"Thank You." As you recall the day, offer thanks to God for the goodness of life and the love that is yours.

"Help me." In those places where you feel inadequate, ask for God's assistance.

"I love you." In spite of failure and inadequacy, you still love God and worship him.

"I'm sorry." Make an honest confession of your mistakes and sin.

Some Helps along the Way

1. **Attend to your life.** Everything that happens to you has meaning. Pay attention to the images that come to you in your meditations on scripture, to your feelings, to the ideas that break into your consciousness with clarity and conviction. Note also the thoughts that you struggle with or reject, the issues in your life that you avoid, and the days you neglect the discipline of reflection altogether.

Notice not only your inner world of thoughts and feelings but also your external world of events—the persons who come into your life, the words spoken to you, the "coincidences" that occur, and the open doors of opportunity. Note a few things each day to "wonder" about.

2. **Discern the Spirit.** Experience will assist you in separating the voice of the Lord from your own unconscious longings. The call of God never conflicts with the Spirit of Jesus Christ; He is the norm for our discernment. The Lord characteristically speaks with gentleness, clarity, persistence, and conviction. The work of the Spirit results in peace. Never make critical changes in your life when you feel confused. When you receive the inner word of the Spirit, look also for confirmation in the external world of persons and events.

3. **Find a Spiritual Friend.** A Spiritual Friend with whom you may talk on a regular basis will make these exercises more meaningful to you. If you are following the directives over a thirty-day period, talk with your friend weekly; if you are making an extended retreat, speak with your friend daily. A Spiritual Friend can ask you helpful questions, offer you support, and pray with you.

4. **Keep a journal.** A journal may be a loose-leaf notebook or a spiral-bound book; or you may choose to write on a computer. The directives suggest meditations and reflections, and they also require the writing of dialogues. To retain your

insights and to preserve your inspirations, write them in a form that you can keep and review. Writing helps formulate your thoughts and externalize them so you can reflect on them. By keeping a record you can review your progress.

5. **Take care of yourself.** If you get "stuck" in a directive you may leave it for a later time; if you encounter feelings with which you cannot cope, be sure to speak with someone who can help. Pay attention to your soul. If you encounter a directive that, for some reason, you cannot follow at the moment, wait until you can. When you do not wish to do a particular directive, reflect on your resistance; get at the source of your avoidance. In some cases you may proceed to the next directive and come back later to the difficult one. Again, these experiences suggest the importance of a spiritual guide.

My prayer is that you will recognize the hand of God as you work through these pages. May God bring clarity and peace as you seek to find and follow God's will.

Ben Campbell Johnson
Professor of Christian Spirituality
Columbia Theological Seminary
Fall 1996

FIRST DIRECTIVE

Recall the Beginning

Everything has had a beginning, but God has always been. As creatures we had a beginning through the generosity of God and in every moment of life we are dependent on our Creator. The Creator graciously shares the gift of being with the creatures and desires their fulfillment in the fulfillment of all things on the earth. Nothing so inspires human gratitude and praise as the awareness of God's eternal goodness and love unrequested.

Psalm 19:1–4: *The heavens are telling the glory of God; and the firmament proclaims his handiwork. Day to day pours forth speech, and night to night declares knowledge. There is no speech, nor are there words; their voice is not heard; yet their voice goes out through all the earth, and their words to the end of the world.*
Almighty God, before the mountains were brought forth or ever you had created the world, even from everlasting to everlasting, you are God. Praise your Name!

Text: Genesis 1:1–26 *In the beginning when God created the heavens and the earth, the earth was a formless void and darkness covered the face of the deep, while a wind from God swept over the face of the waters. Then God said, "Let there be light"; and there was light. And God saw that the light was good; and God separated the light from the darkness. God called the light Day, and the darkness he called Night. And there was evening and there was morning, the first day.*
And God said, "Let there be a dome in the midst of the waters, and let it separate the waters from the waters." So God

13

made the dome and separated the waters that were under the dome from the waters that were above the dome. And it was so. God called the dome Sky. And there was evening and there was morning, the second day. And God said, "Let the waters under the sky be gathered together into one place, and let the dry land appear." And it was so. God called the dry land Earth, and the waters that were gathered together he called Seas. And God saw that it was good.

Then God said, "Let the earth put forth vegetation: plants yielding seed, and fruit trees of every kind on earth that bear fruit with the seed in it." And it was so.

The earth brought forth vegetation: plants yielding seed of every kind, and trees of every kind bearing fruit with the seed in it. And God saw that it was good. And there was evening and there was morning, the third day.

And God said, "Let there be lights in the dome of the sky to separate the day from the night; and let them be for signs and for seasons and for days and years, and let them be lights in the dome of the sky to give light upon the earth." And it was so. God made the two great lights—the greater light to rule the day and the lesser light to rule the night—and the stars. God set them in the dome of the sky to give light upon the earth, to rule over the day and over the night, and to separate the light from the darkness. And God saw that it was good. And there was evening and there was morning, the fourth day.

And God said, "Let the waters bring forth swarms of living creatures, and let birds fly above the earth across the dome of the sky." So God created the great sea monsters and every living creature that moves, of every kind, with which the waters swarm, and every winged bird of every kind. And God saw that it was good. God blessed them, saying, "Be fruitful and multiply and fill the waters in the seas, and let birds multiply on the earth." And there was evening and there was morning, the fifth day.

And God said, "Let the earth bring forth living creatures of *every kind: cattle and creeping things and wild animals of the earth of every kind." And it was so.*

God made the wild animals of the earth of every kind, and the cattle of every kind, and everything that creeps upon the ground of every kind. And God saw that it was good.

Then God said, "Let us make humankind in our image, according to our likeness; and let them have dominion over the fish of the sea, and over the birds of the air, and over the cattle, and over all the wild animals of the earth, and over every creeping thing that creeps upon the earth."

Guide to the text:

1. As you read the story of creation try to imagine that you are present at the beginning, watching it happen. (Take twenty or thirty minutes to visualize the happenings detailed in the text.)

2. Notice the repetition of the words *And God said.* What follows this phrase?

3. Spend time thinking about the goodness of the Creator and the goodness of creation.

4. In your journal make a list of the thoughts and feelings that come to you as you think about the beginning of all things in God.

Alternative guide to the text:

Read this text slowly. Place yourself as a witness to Creation. Attend to the thoughts, images, and feelings that come to you. Meditate on the gracious beginning of all things until you are filled with wonder and awe.

Gracious God, in your benevolence you chose not to remain alone in your beauty, goodness, and perfection, but you called a world into being wherein you would work out your purposes. Praise to your Name!

SECOND DIRECTIVE

Accept Your Creaturehood!

God made humans unique among all creatures on earth. We are aware of our beginning and our end. The time we have been given, the place we have been set, and the gifts we possess define our destiny. Created in the image of God for the purposes of God, we either fulfill God's will or deny it. "The chief end of humanity is to glorify God and to enjoy this God forever!" No human agenda can be substituted for this divine intention.

Psalm: 8:1–9: *O LORD, our Sovereign, how majestic is your name in all the earth! You have set your glory above the heavens. Out of the mouths of babes and infants you have founded a bulwark because of your foes, to silence the enemy and the avenger.*

When I look at your heavens, the work of your fingers, the moon and the stars that you have established; what are human beings that you are mindful of them, mortals that you care for them? Yet you have made them a little lower than God, and crowned them with glory and honor. You have given them dominion over the works of your hands; you have put all things under their feet, all sheep and oxen, and also the beasts of the field, the birds of the air, and the fish of the sea, whatever passes along the paths of the seas.

O LORD, our Sovereign, how majestic is your name in all the earth!

O God, you have made me like yourself and nothing less than yourself can satisfy the cravings of my spirit. I seek you that I may know you and be known by you.

Text: Genesis 1:26–31 *Then God said, "Let us make humankind in our image, according to our likeness; and let them have dominion over the fish of the sea, and over the birds of the air, and over the cattle, and over all the wild animals of the earth, and over every creeping thing that creeps upon the earth."*

So God created humankind in his image, in the image of God he created them; male and female he created them. God blessed them, and God said to them, "Be fruitful and multiply, and fill the earth and subdue it; and have dominion over the fish of the sea and over the birds of the air and over every living thing that moves upon the earth."

God said, "See, I have given you every plant yielding seed that is upon the face of all the earth, and every tree with seed in its fruit; you shall have them for food. And to every beast of the earth, and to every bird of the air, and to everything that creeps on the earth, everything that has the breath of life, I have given every green plant for food." And it was so.

God saw everything that he had made, and indeed, it was very good. And there was evening and there was morning, the sixth day.

Guide to the text:
1. Reflect on the introductory paragraph above.
2. Meditate on the nature of a Creator who would give you the privilege of participating in the divine purpose. (See Introduction for help with meditation.)
3. Think on the fact that you are made in the image of the eternal God and have been destined to participate in God's plan. What does being in the image of God mean to you?
4. In succession, focus your awareness on each of the following statements. Repeat each affirmation slowly in rhythm with your breathing and notice the thoughts and feelings each affirmation elicits. (Write your thoughts.)

"I was always in God's mind..."
"I was made in the image of God..."
"I am alive and conscious of my being..."
"I will be involved with God in all my life..."
"I will be forever..."

5. After spending time with the text in the ways suggested above, write a letter to God in which you describe as fully as you can the issues in your life in which you need discernment. State what you would like for God to reveal to you as you proceed with these directives. (Review this letter from time to time to note the progress being made.)

Alternative guide to the text:

After reading the text, quieting yourself, and reflecting on "being made in the image of God," draw a picture or create a symbol that expresses your desire to have your being directed toward the will of God.

In meditation on the hunger for God's will, images often surface in our minds. It will assist you on your journey to project them onto paper in the form of pictures or sketches.

As clearly as you can, describe your need for discerning the will of God. From time to time return to this statement and review your progress.

Creator God, I am wonderfully and fearfully made, and I do not fully understand all the faculties that have been given me to know you and to do your will. Show me who I am and what I am to do with my life.

THIRD DIRECTIVE

Face Yourself Honestly

Sin disrupts God's plan, offends God's holiness, and keeps us from rejoicing in the Lord's presence. Choosing our own will instead of God's not only takes away our joy, it perverts our life. From the rejection of God's will stems human pain, destructiveness, and meaninglessness. Tragically, all humans participate in this misery of the "fall."

Psalm 5:3–6, 9–11: *O LORD, in the morning you hear my voice; in the morning I plead my case to you, and watch. For you are not a God who delights in wickedness; evil will not sojourn with you. The boastful will not stand before your eyes; you hate all evildoers. You destroy those who speak lies; the LORD abhors the bloodthirsty and deceitful...*

For there is no truth in their mouths; their hearts are destruction; their throats are open graves; they flatter with their tongues. Make them bear their guilt, O God; let them fall by their own counsels; because of their many transgressions cast them out, for they have rebelled against you. But let all who take refuge in you rejoice; let them ever sing for joy. Spread your protection over them, so that those who love your name may exult in you.

0 God, show me the condition of my heart that causes me to turn away from you and to seek my own will instead of yours. Let me experience in your presence the exact nature of my sinfulness and the fear that turns me away from you.

Text: Genesis 3:1–13 *Now the serpent was more crafty than any other wild animal that the LORD God had made. He said* to the woman, "Did God say, 'You shall not eat from any tree in the garden'?"

The woman said to the serpent, "We may eat of the fruit of the trees in the garden; but God said, 'You shall not eat of the fruit of the tree that is in the middle of the garden, nor shall you touch it, or you shall die.'"

But the serpent said to the woman, "You will not die; for God knows that when you eat of it your eyes will be opened, and you will be like God, knowing good and evil."

So when the woman saw that the tree was good for food, and that it was a delight to the eyes, and that the tree was to be desired to make one wise, she took of its fruit and ate; and she also gave some to her husband, who was with her, and he ate. Then the eyes of both were opened, and they knew that they were naked; and they sewed fig leaves together and made loincloths for themselves. They heard the sound of the LORD God walking in the garden at the time of the evening breeze, and the man and his wife hid themselves from the presence of the LORD God among the trees of the garden.

But the LORD God called to the man, and said to him, "Where are you?"

He said, "I heard the sound of you in the garden, and I was afraid, because I was naked; and I hid myself."

He said, "Who told you that you were naked? Have you eaten from the tree of which I commanded you not to eat?"

The man said, "The woman whom you gave to be with me, she gave me fruit from the tree, and I ate."

Then the LORD God said to the woman, "What is this that you have done?" The woman said, "The serpent tricked me, and I ate."

Guide to the text:
1. Fix in your mind the different scenes described in the text.
2. Imagine yourself to be present in the garden. Close your

eyes, picture the unfolding events and the conversations that occur. Visualize these events as one present and seeing them. Give special attention to the suggestions of the serpent.

3. Shift your attention from the "fall" of our first parents to your own "fall," your own garden of innocence and the first conscious temptation to which you yielded. Where were you? What was the exact nature of the temptation? What satisfaction did it promise? What were the consequences?

4. Write an account of your fall that includes the nature of your temptation, the choice to yield, and the consequences of your choice as it affected your feelings about yourself, others, and God.

5. From this one experience what do you learn about the nature and consequence of sin?

Alternative guide to the text:
Notice each aspect of the temptation of our first parents in the garden. Recall your first "fall" from innocence. Write the dialogue that took place in your mind as you were dealing with the first temptation. (This dialogue becomes a narrative of your fall and expulsion from the garden.)

O Lord God, my heart is deceitful above all things and terribly weak. Help me to know my heart. Have mercy on me for I am a sinner in need of your kindness.

FOURTH DIRECTIVE

Acknowledge Your True Condition

Though broken and sinful, we are not hopeless. Turning from God's will to our own will is the essence of sin. The law of God reveals to us the nature of God and the nature of our sins. No healing of our lives can occur until we honestly own our sins and confess them to God. God has promised to forgive our sins and to restore us to a relation with God. Because of God's unconditional love, we have the courage to be totally honest about our sins; and because of God's promise to forgive, we dare to confess our sins and to believe we are restored to the family of God.

Psalm 19:7–10: *The law of the LORD is perfect, reviving the soul; the decrees of the LORD are sure, making wise the simple; the precepts of the LORD are right, rejoicing the heart; the commandment of the LORD is clear, enlightening the eyes; the fear of the LORD is pure, enduring forever; the ordinances of the LORD are true and righteous altogether. More to be desired are they than gold, even much fine gold; sweeter also than honey, and drippings of the honeycomb.*

O God, make me aware of the exact nature of my sins and give me the courage to acknowledge them both to myself and to you.

Text: Exodus 20:1–17 *Then God spoke all these words: I am the LORD your God, who brought you out of the land of Egypt, out of the house of slavery; you shall have no other gods before me. You shall not make for yourself an idol, whether in the form of* *anything that is in heaven above, or that is on the earth beneath, or that is in the water under the earth.*

You shall not bow down to them or worship them; for I the LORD your God am a jealous God, punishing children for the iniquity of parents, to the third and the fourth generation of those who reject me, but showing steadfast love to the thousandth generation of those who love me and keep my commandments.

You shall not make wrongful use of the name of the LORD your God, for the LORD will not acquit anyone who misuses his name.

Remember the sabbath day, and keep it holy.

Six days you shall labor and do all your work. But the seventh day is a sabbath to the LORD your God; you shall not do any work—you, your son or your daughter, your male or female slave, your livestock, or the alien resident in your towns. For in six days the LORD made heaven and earth, the sea, and all that is in them, but rested the seventh day; therefore the LORD blessed the sabbath day and consecrated it.

Honor your father and your mother, so that your days may be long in the land that the LORD your God is giving you.

You shall not murder.

You shall not commit adultery.

You shall not steal.

You shall not bear false witness against your neighbor.

You shall not covet your neighbor's house; you shall not covet your neighbor's wife, or male or female slave, or ox, or donkey, or anything that belongs to your neighbor.

Guide to the text:

1. Read the commands of God. After reading each, recall the specific ways you have broken the command. Make a list of your sins. (You may not wish to record these in your journal. Perhaps a separate piece of paper will suffice.)
2. The thoughtful review of your life in light of the commandments of God will probably take more than one day.

This is important but painful work. Take the time you require to be thorough.

3. Before you begin making this list of your sins, read the story of the Expectant Father (Lk 15:11–32) and hold before you this image of the Loving God to whom you make your confession.

4. When you have completed the list of sins committed, name each one separately and pray: "Lord, be merciful to me, a sinner."

Alternative guide to the text:

Think over your entire life from your first consciousness of sin to the present and on a sheet of paper write a word or phrase that represents those sins that most bother you. Wad the paper. Place it in your cupped hands. Ask for God's forgiveness. Burn the paper outside in the open air and watch the smoke of your confession rise and disappear. "Thanks be to God."

Lord God, I can acknowledge the truth of my condition before you only because of a sure confidence that you love me in spite of my sin.

FIFTH DIRECTIVE

Examine Your Heart

Jesus Christ mirrors God's perfect intention for us. In him we see a reflection of God and a representation of true humanity. His life and suffering and death expose the depth of human sinfulness, and his words teach us the goals for our lives. St. Paul realized that the power of sin not only corrupts our behavior but also stains our hearts, so we must examine our hearts as well as our actions.

Psalm 51:1–7, 10–12: *Have mercy on me, O God, according to your steadfast love; according to your abundant mercy blot out my transgressions. Wash me thoroughly from my iniquity, and cleanse me from my sin. For I know my transgressions, and my sin is ever before me. Against you, you alone, have I sinned, and done what is evil in your sight, so that you are justified in your sentence and blameless when you pass judgment. Indeed, I was born guilty, a sinner when my mother conceived me. You desire truth in the inward being; therefore teach me wisdom in my secret heart. Purge me with hyssop, and I shall be clean; wash me, and I shall be whiter than snow....Create in me a clean heart, O God, and put a new and right spirit within me. Do not cast me away from your presence, and do not take your holy spirit from me. Restore to me the joy of your salvation, and sustain in me a willing spirit.*

O God, help me to know my heart that I may confess to you my impulses and intentions as well as my actions. I long to find healing for my perverse will as well as forgiveness for my past actions through Jesus Christ my Lord. Grant me a clean heart and a pure life, I pray.

Text: Romans 12:9–21 *Let love be genuine; hate what is evil, hold fast to what is good; love one another with mutual affection; outdo one another in showing honor. Do not lag in zeal, be ardent in spirit, serve the Lord. Rejoice in hope, be patient in suffering, persevere in prayer. Contribute to the needs of the saints; extend hospitality to strangers. Bless those who persecute you; bless and do not curse them. Rejoice with those who rejoice, weep with those who weep. Live in harmony with one another; do not be haughty, but associate with the lowly; do not claim to be wiser than you are. Do not repay anyone evil for evil, but take thought for what is noble in the sight of all. If it is possible, so far as it depends on you, live peaceably with all. Beloved, never avenge yourselves, but leave room for the wrath of God; for it is written, "Vengeance is mine, I will repay, says the Lord." No, "if your enemies are hungry, feed them; if they are thirsty, give them something to drink; for by doing this you will heap burning coals on their heads." Do not be overcome by evil, but overcome evil with good.*

Guide to the text:
1. Reflect on each of the admonitions of St. Paul. Make a list of the places at which you fall short.
2. Review this list of sins while considering the seriousness of each and the pain that it has brought to Christ.
3. Own your sinfulness without apology or excuse.
4. List each of St. Paul's admonitions and indicate a specific way that you can put his guidance into practice. Begin today building the habit of living in this new way of life.
5. Visualize Jesus inviting you, "Come unto me all you who labor and are heavy laden and I will give you rest. Take my yoke upon you and learn of me for I am meek and lowly in heart and you will find rest for your soul, for my yoke is easy and my burden is light." (Mt 11:28–30) Meditate on this invitation as it applies to your shortcomings.

Alternative guide to the text:

Set aside one hour to be in the presence of God. Focus on the figure of Jesus on the cross. Empty yourself of all trivial thoughts, feelings, and desires. Let yourself sit before God. Permit God to manifest himself to you in the manner that God chooses.

Holy God, let me this day feel in my mind and body the depth of pain that my sin causes, so that I may come to hate sin as you do.

SIXTH DIRECTIVE

Accept the Forgiveness of God

The depth of human sinfulness drives us to God, who not only condemns but also forgives sin. To forgive our sins this holy God has personally taken in the pain of our rebellion. Having received Christ's sacrifice for our sins, God forgives our offenses and erases the memory of our transgressions. In this gracious act God restores us to full membership in the family. The mercy of God extends to the worst sinner, offering pardon and hope.

Psalm 32:1–5, 11: *Happy are those whose transgression is forgiven, whose sin is covered. Happy are those to whom the LORD imputes no iniquity, and in whose spirit there is no deceit. While I kept silence, my body wasted away through my groaning all day long. For day and night your hand was heavy upon me; my strength was dried up as by the heat of summer. Then I acknowledged my sin to you, and I did not hide my iniquity; I said, "I will confess my transgressions to the LORD," and you forgave the guilt of my sin...*
Be glad in the LORD and rejoice, O righteous, and shout for joy, all you upright in heart.

O Lord, I confess to you all the sins of my life that I may find in your mercy both forgiveness and healing through Christ. Hear my prayer and make me whole.

Text: Luke 19:9–14 *Then Jesus said to him, "Today salvation has come to this house, because he too is a son of Abraham. For the Son of Man came to seek out and to save the lost." As they were listening to this, he went on to tell a parable, because he was near*

28

Jerusalem, and because they supposed that the kingdom of God was to appear immediately. So he said, "A nobleman went to a distant country to get royal power for himself and then return. He summoned ten of his slaves, and gave them ten pounds, and said to them, 'Do business with these until I come back.' But the citizens of his country hated him and sent a delegation after him, saying, 'We do not want this man to rule over us.'"

Guide to the text:

1. Review the acknowledgments of sin in your life that you have recorded in the previous two directives.
2. Name each sin and, after each, repeat the tax collector's prayer: "God, be merciful to me a sinner."
3. Repeat this promise of God: *"If we confess our sins, he who is faithful and just will forgive us our sins and cleanse us from all unrighteousness."* (I John 1:9) Tear up the pages with your lists of sins, burn them in a fire, or flush them. They are gone forever.
4. Sit quietly before the Lord. Listen to his word to you. Write the thoughts that come to you after releasing your sins.
5. Imagine engaging life without the burden of past guilt and failure.
6. Write a letter to God expressing your feelings. Include in your letter your hopes for the future.

Alternative guide to the text:

Find one person whom you can trust with your confession. Ask for permission to tell him or her the sins and failures that bother you. When you have finished your confession, request that the listener read these words to you: "If we confess our sins, he is faithful and just to forgive us our sins and to cleanse us from all unrighteousness."

Lord, thank you for hearing my confession, for forgiving my sin, and for healing my brokenness. Teach me to live wholly for you.

SEVENTH DIRECTIVE

Listen for Christ

A forgiven heart left empty becomes the target for both old and new sins. Once forgiven we must reorient our lives to the divine plan. As part of our turning around we arise and walk in the power of Christ. God desires to lead us in what we are to do and who we are to become. The will of God has been written both in scripture and in the flesh of our hearts. To fulfill our destiny we must listen for guidance from the word without and the Spirit within.

Psalm 13:1–6: *How long, O LORD? Will you forget me forever? How long will you hide your face from me? How long must I bear pain in my soul, and have sorrow in my heart all day long? How long shall my enemy be exalted over me? Consider and answer me, O LORD my God! Give light to my eyes, or I will sleep the sleep of death, and my enemy will say, "I have prevailed"; my foes will rejoice because I am shaken. But I trusted in your steadfast love; my heart shall rejoice in your salvation. I will sing to the LORD, because he has dealt bountifully with me.*

O God, fill my mind and imagination with images of your divine purpose for me so that I may be guided to fulfill your eternal purpose for my one and only life.

Text: Mark 2:1–12 *When he returned to Capernaum after some days, it was reported that he was at home. So many gathered around that there was no longer room for them, not even in front of the door; and he was speaking the word to them. Then some people came, bringing to him a paralyzed man, carried by four of them. And when they could not bring him to Jesus because of the*

*crowd, they removed the roof above him; and after having dug
through it, they let down the mat on which the paralytic lay.
When Jesus saw their faith, he said to the paralytic, "Son, your
sins are forgiven." Now some of the scribes were sitting there,
questioning in their hearts, "Why does this fellow speak in this
way? It is blasphemy! Who can forgive sins but God alone?" At
once Jesus perceived in his spirit that they were discussing these
questions among themselves; and he said to them, "Why do you
raise such questions in your hearts? Which is easier, to say to the
paralytic, 'Your sins are forgiven,' or to say, 'Stand up and take
your mat and walk'? But so that you may know that the Son of
Man has authority on earth to forgive sins"—he said to the paralytic—"I say to you, stand up, take your mat and go to your
home." And he stood up, and immediately took the mat and
went out before all of them; so that they were all amazed and glo-
rified God, saying, "We have never seen anything like this!"*

Guide to the text:

1. Read the story of the healing and underline the different
    persons or groups of persons who are present.
2. Choose one of these persons or groups with whom you
    can partially identify (e.g., the paralytic, a scribe, etc.).
3. Read the text again and view the occurrence from the
    perspective of the character you have chosen. Close your
    eyes and replay the entire event. Be silent in the presence
    of the healing.
4. Write a page or two telling this story from the perspective
    of the person with whom you have identified. Write in
    first person and add imaginative details.
5. Imagine that all the persons have gone. You are left alone
    with Christ. Ask him the question that seems to come
    naturally to you. Record his answer. Continue writing the
    dialogue as long as any thoughts come to you. (See Intro-
    duction for help in writing your dialogue.)

6. Reflect on what you have written. What do you discover about yourself? About Christ?
7. Read your letter of request in the Second Directive and reflect on your progress in discernment. Revise the letter if your requests have changed.

Alternative guide to the text:

Imagine that you are one of the four persons who took the paralytic to Jesus. Write a first-person account of your experience beginning with the time when the idea came to you to take your friend to Jesus.

Creator God, create within me the Spirit of Jesus so that his life may be manifested in my daily life.

EIGHTH DIRECTIVE

Be Conformed to Christ

Jesus Christ, the will of God made visible and tangible, reveals to us the hidden intention for our life. To receive his revelation we look at his life, listen to his words, and wait in his presence. In the silence we listen for his voice so that we may respond to his call. The stories and sayings of Jesus make possible our encounter with his Spirit here and now. Through disciples like us he continues his work. He calls us today and directs our lives!

Psalm 53:1–4, 6: *Fools say in their hearts, "There is no God." They are corrupt, they commit abominable acts; there is no one who does good. God looks down from heaven on humankind to see if there are any who are wise, who seek after God.*

They have all fallen away, they are all alike perverse; there is no one who does good, no, not one. Have they no knowledge, those evildoers, who eat up my people as they eat bread, and do not call upon God?... Oh, that deliverance for Israel would come from Zion! When God restores the fortunes of his people, Jacob will rejoice; Israel will be glad.

Lord Jesus, open my eyes to the mystery of your coming into the world and grant that I may recognize your coming today and your call to your disciple.

Text: Luke 1:26–38 *In the sixth month the angel Gabriel was sent by God to a town in Galilee called Nazareth, to a virgin engaged to a man whose name was Joseph, of the house of David. The virgin's name was Mary. And he came to her and said, "Greetings, favored one! The Lord is with you." But she was*

33

much perplexed by his words and pondered what sort of greeting this might be. The angel said to her, "Do not be afraid, Mary, for you have found favor with God. And now, you will conceive in your womb and bear a son, and you will name him Jesus. He will be great, and will be called the Son of the Most High, and the Lord God will give to him the throne of his ancestor David. He will reign over the house of Jacob forever, and of his kingdom there will be no end." Mary said to the angel, "How can this be, since I am a virgin?" The angel said to her, "The Holy Spirit will come upon you, and the power of the Most High will overshadow you; therefore the child to be born will be holy; he will be called Son of God.

"And now, your relative Elizabeth in her old age has also conceived a son; and this is the sixth month for her who was said to be barren. For nothing will be impossible with God." Then Mary said, "Here am I, the servant of the Lord; let it be with me according to your word." Then the angel departed from her.

Guide to the text:

1. Visualize the encounter between Mary and Gabriel—the place, time of day, Mary's emotions, her experience, and her concerns.
2. Meditate on the words of the angel to Mary and her responses. (See the Introduction for help with meditation.)
3. Imagine yourself in Mary's role and write an account of the angel's visit. (Think of the account as an entry in her diary.) Be sure to include her feelings, fears, and questions.
4. As you think of the angel's visit to Mary, what images and associations do you make in your own life? How are Christ and his will being conceived in your life?
5. Write a prayer that arises from the realization that his will is being conceived in you today.

Alternative guide to the text:

With a pen or crayon draw a symbol that represents your vision of God becoming human in Jesus. Ponder this mystery as it relates to the divine becoming flesh in you. Record the thoughts that come to you. (Remember that as you begin to write, the act itself helps you to express thoughts that you have not had before.)

O Christ, come to me, abide with me, be conceived in me today!

NINTH DIRECTIVE

Contemplate the Divine Made Human

The invisible God has become visible in Jesus Christ. The divine mystery for which humans groped through the centuries chose to be disclosed in human flesh. God came into history in a form that revealed the divine nature and purpose without destroying the humanity of Jesus or our humanity. The Lord God transforms our lives while respecting our freedom.

Psalm 2:7–9: *I will tell of the decree of the LORD: He said to me, "You are my son; today I have begotten you. Ask of me, and I will make the nations your heritage, and the ends of the earth your possession. You shall break them with a rod of iron, and dash them in pieces like a potter's vessel."*

O Christ, Word of God, give me ears to hear you speak of the intention of God for the world and for my place in it.

Text: John 1:1–5, 14–18 *In the beginning was the Word, and the Word was with God, and the Word was God. He was in the beginning with God. All things came into being through him, and without him not one thing came into being. What has come into being in him was life, and the life was the light of all people. The light shines in the darkness, and the darkness did not overcome it.... And the Word became flesh and lived among us, and we have seen his glory, the glory as of a father's only son, full of grace and truth. (John testified to him and cried out, "This was he of whom I said, 'He who comes after me ranks ahead of me because he was before me.'") From his fullness we have all received, grace upon grace. The law indeed was given through Moses; grace and truth came through Jesus Christ. No one has* *ever seen God. It is God the only Son, who is close to the Father's heart, who has made him known.*

Guide to the text:

1. Read the text slowly, thinking deeply about the incarnation of the eternal Word of God.
2. Close your eyes and sit before the mystery of God becoming human! Attend the images and ideas that come to you. Follow your thoughts wherever they lead you. Listen for the voice of God in the silence.
3. Record the images and ideas that made the strongest impression on you during your silence. Use these ideas to enter into prayer.
4. In your prayer ask that the Spirit reveal to you how the coming of God in Jesus reveals God's intention for your life today. Write in your journal any thoughts that come to you.

Alternative guide to the text:

Describe how God's becoming flesh in Jesus provides a model for his becoming flesh in us.

Write a prayer that expresses your desire, anxiety, hope, or doubt about God's becoming flesh in you.

O Word of God made flesh, in you I am faced with God's will made visible. As I open my mind and heart to your divine presence, reshape me according to your divine intention.

TENTH DIRECTIVE

Consider the Mystery of Birth

Spiritual life like natural life begins with birth. We do not, cannot fully understand the mystery of our beginning. God spoke and it was done; God commanded and life came forth. In the mystery of Christ's birth resides both the power and the substance of our rebirth. His birth in Bethlehem provides a model for his birth in human hearts in every age. A birth means new life, a new beginning, and new opportunities.

Psalm 22:9–11: *Yet it was you who took me from the womb; you kept me safe on my mother's breast. On you I was cast from my birth, and since my mother bore me you have been my God. Do not be far from me, for trouble is near and there is no one to help.*

O Christ, your birth as a human being shows how the divine presence comes into human flesh and unites with it. May your divine Spirit prepare me to recognize and to receive the coming of God's holy will.

Text: Luke 2:1–7 *In those days a decree went out from Emperor Augustus that all the world should be registered. This was the first registration and was taken while Quirinius was governor of Syria. All went to their own towns to be registered. Joseph also went from the town of Nazareth in Galilee to Judea, to the city of David called Bethlehem, because he was descended from the house and family of David. He went to be registered with Mary, to whom he was engaged and who was expecting a child. While they were there, the time came for her to deliver her child. And she gave birth to her firstborn son and wrapped him*

in bands of cloth, and laid him in a manger, because there was
no place for them in the inn.

Guide to the text:
1. Imagine yourself in the stable in Bethlehem. Visualize the occurrences that surround the birth of Jesus as though you are there as a participant.
2. Meditate on the phrase "the time came for her to deliver." How do you associate your life and God's intention with this event?
3. If your consciousness is the womb in which Christ and his will are conceived, how would God's will be born in you today?
4. Write an account of the birth in your consciousness of the concern you have for his will.
5. Write a prayer expressing your gratitude for his love for you.

Alternative guide to the text:
Find a picture of the Nativity. Gaze at it for a long time.
Record the thoughts that come to you about Christ's coming into
the world then and his coming into your life now.

O Christ, you were conceived in a strange womb, born in a borrowed room, but you attracted attention far and near. Let your presence be born in me today; make my pathway clear.

ELEVENTH DIRECTIVE

Enter the Mystery of Baptism

In his baptism Jesus fully identified himself with sinful human beings. In baptism we are joined to Christ, to all the members of his body on earth, and to the needs of humanity whom he came to save. Through baptism we have confidence that our past has been forgiven and our future has new possibilities. The memory of our baptism into Christ renews in us the enduring reality of reconciliation with God, our fellow humans, and the whole of creation. Baptism is the tangible evidence of God's decision for us.

Psalm 25:6–10: *Be mindful of your mercy, O LORD, and of your steadfast love, for they have been from of old. Do not remember the sins of my youth or my transgressions; according to your steadfast love remember me, for your goodness' sake, O LORD! Good and upright is the LORD; therefore he instructs sinners in the way. He leads the humble in what is right, and teaches the humble his way. All the paths of the LORD are steadfast love and faithfulness, for those who keep his covenant and his decrees.*

Loving Father, let me hear you speak to me those words of confirmation that you spoke to your only begotten: "You are my beloved son, with you I am well pleased."

Text: Matthew 3:13–17 *Then Jesus came from Galilee to John at the Jordan, to be baptized by him. John would have prevented him, saying, "I need to be baptized by you, and do you come to me?" But Jesus answered him, "Let it be so now; for it is proper for us in this way to fulfill all righteousness." Then he consented. And when Jesus had been baptized, just as he came*

40

up from the water, suddenly the heavens were opened to him and he saw the Spirit of God descending like a dove and alighting on him. And a voice from heaven said, "This is my Son, the Beloved, with whom I am well pleased."

Guide to the text:

1. Imagine that you stand among the crowd at Jesus' baptism. Visualize the incident: Who is present? What is the landscape? The weather? Include sights, sounds, taste, touch, and smells. Write a first-person report of what occurred.

2. Repeat the meditation except this time place yourself in the role of Jesus and especially attend the words spoken to Jesus: "You are my beloved son (daughter), with you I am well pleased."

3. What feelings do you have about being a child of God? God's being pleased with you?

4. Write a response to God, who says to you, "You are my much loved son (daughter), with you I am well pleased." Continue writing the dialogue.

Alternative guide to the text:

Fill a bowl with water. Generously pour or sprinkle it over yourself while saying, "I am baptized into Jesus Christ." Continue to claim the meaning of your baptism. Place your hand on your head and say, "I have been baptized. With me God is well pleased. In Christ, God's will for me has been made known."

After performing this renewal, record your reflections on it.

Gracious God, because I am loved by you and you are pleased with me, guide me into your will for my life.

TWELFTH DIRECTIVE

Persevere in Temptation

Jesus was tested in every way possible—fulfillment of bodily needs, pride of a special relationship with God, and lust for this world's goods. In all these tests Adam and Eve, our first parents, failed, but Christ remained firm in his obedience to God. The Lord tests every child to prove our faithfulness and to season our faith. Followers of Jesus should never be shocked by the testing of the Lord.

Psalm 3:1–6: *O LORD, how many are my foes! Many are rising against me; many are saying to me, "There is no help for you in God." but you, O LORD, are a shield around me, my glory, and the one who lifts up my head. I cry aloud to the LORD, and he answers me from his holy hill. I lie down and sleep; I wake again, for the LORD sustains me. I am not afraid of ten thousands of people who have set themselves against me all around.*

Lord Jesus, since you have been tempted in every way possible to humans, grant me the strength to withstand temptation and the courage to trust in your purpose.

Text: Matthew 4:1–11 *Then Jesus was led up by the Spirit into the wilderness to be tempted by the devil. He fasted forty days and forty nights, and afterwards he was famished. The tempter came and said to him, "If you are the Son of God, command these stones to become loaves of bread." But he answered, "It is written, 'One does not live by bread alone, but by every word that comes from the mouth of God.'" Then the devil took him to the holy city and placed him on the pinnacle of the temple,* *saying to him, "If you are the Son of God, throw yourself down; for it is written, 'He will command his angels concerning you,' and 'On their hands they will bear you up, so that you will not dash your foot against a stone.'" Jesus said to him, "Again it is written, 'Do not put the Lord your God to the test.'" Again, the devil took him to a very high mountain and showed him all the kingdoms of the world and their splendor; and he said to him, "All these I will give you, if you will fall down and worship me." Jesus said to him, "Away with you, Satan! for it is written, 'Worship the Lord your God, and serve only him.'" Then the devil left him, and suddenly angels came and waited on him.*

Guide to the text:
1. Read this text against the background of the baptism.
2. What were the tests put to Jesus? How do these tests come to you today?
3. Place yourself in the desert. Use all your senses to acclimate yourself to the setting for the temptation.
4. Imagine yourself on a huge rock listening to the devil's temptations and to Jesus' responses. Write a firsthand report of the event (using the suggestions for journaling found in the Introduction).
5. Write a prayer requesting help in the temptations that you now face regarding God's purpose for your life.

Alternative guide to the text:
Bend a wire (coat hanger, etc.) to symbolize your present testing or temptation. When you have finished bending the wire, gaze at it for several minutes. Record in your journal any reflections that you have regarding the temptation. Record your insights and the determinations you are making.

Lord Jesus, daily I am tempted to turn from your call through desires that arise from my passions, pride, and lust for power. Grant me in my temptations the power to say no to sin and yes to your will.

THIRTEENTH DIRECTIVE

Listen for His Call

Just as Jesus walked by the seaside in the first century calling fishermen to follow him, he walks the byways of our lives calling us to follow him in our day. He calls us to fulfill his mission, the mission of God in the world. His call simultaneously fulfills his will and also our lives. Following him begins with a single step, the first one. He gives us strength and courage to follow him, one step at a time, one day at a time.

Psalm 114:1–6: *When Israel went out from Egypt, the house of Jacob from a people of strange language, Judah became God's sanctuary, Israel his dominion. The sea looked and fled; Jordan turned back. The mountains skipped like rams, the hills like lambs. Why is it, O sea, that you flee? O Jordan, that you turn back? O mountains, that you skip like rams? O hills, like lambs?*

O Christ, whose call is continuous, grant me attentive ears that I may hear your summons to the meaning of my life and the task you have for me to do.

Text: Matthew 4:18–22 *As he walked by the Sea of Galilee, he saw two brothers, Simon, who is called Peter, and Andrew his brother, casting a net into the sea—for they were fishermen. And he said to them, "Follow me, and I will make you fish for people." Immediately they left their nets and followed him. As he went from there, he saw two other brothers, James son of Zebedee and his brother John, in the boat with their father, Zebedee, mending their nets, and he called them. Immediately they left the boat and their father, and followed him.*

Guide to the text:

1. Prepare yourself to meet Christ through the text. (See Preparation for Meditation in the Introduction.)
2. Review the events depicted in these texts using all your senses to participate in the meeting with Jesus and his subsequent call.
3. Imagine that you are Andrew. Write a first-person reflection on your experiences of being with John the Baptist, hearing his testimony to Jesus, following Jesus home, talking with him, returning for Simon, and then hearing his call to you beside the sea. Your reflection should include your questions, fears, delights, and hopes.
4. Review your reflection and underline the words and phrases that describe you as well as Andrew.
5. Ponder the question: "To what does Jesus seem to be calling me?"
6. Write a prayer in which you ask for the appropriate grace to overcome each fear you have in responding to his call.

Alternative guide to the text:

Talk with a trusted friend about the sense of call from Christ that is coming to you. Listen carefully to what this person says to you. Record your reflections on the conversation.

Lord Jesus, grant me the strength and courage to obey your call so that I may honor the Father, further your mission, and fulfill your will for my life.

FOURTEENTH DIRECTIVE

Learn to Pray

Prayer opens us more deeply to the call of God and provides a relationship in which our perception of the call may be clarified. In prayer the human cry for guidance meets with the divine desire to lead us. Prayer purifies human desires so that the divine will can be known more clearly. True prayer becomes a dialogue in which listening is often more important than speaking. Christ the Teacher abides in us to instruct us in this art.

Psalm 61:1–5: *Hear my cry, O God; listen to my prayer. From the end of the earth I call to you, when my heart is faint. Lead me to the rock that is higher than I; for you are my refuge, a strong tower against the enemy. Let me abide in your tent forever, find refuge under the shelter of your wings. For you, O God, have heard my vows; you have given me the heritage of those who fear your name.*

Lord Jesus, as of old you taught your followers to pray, teach me also to pray. Make your call clear to me that I may joyously obey you.

Text: Luke 11:1–11 *He was praying in a certain place, and after he had finished, one of his disciples said to him, "Lord, teach us to pray, as John taught his disciples." He said to them, "When you pray, say: Father, hallowed be your name. Your kingdom come. Give us each day our daily bread. And forgive us our sins, for we ourselves forgive everyone indebted to us. And do not bring us to the time of trial."*
And he said to them, "Suppose one of you has a friend, and

*you go to him at midnight and say to him, 'Friend, lend me
three loaves of bread; for a friend of mine has arrived, and I
have nothing to set before him.' And he answers from within,
'Do not bother me; the door has already been locked, and my
children are with me in bed; I cannot get up and give you anything.' I tell you, even though he will not get up and give him
anything because he is his friend, at least because of his persistence he will get up and give him whatever he needs.*

*"So I say to you, Ask, and it will be given you; search, and you
will find; knock, and the door will be opened for you. For everyone who asks receives, and everyone who searches finds, and for
everyone who knocks, the door will be opened. Is there anyone
among you who, if your child asks for a fish, will give a snake
instead of a fish? Or if the child asks for an egg, will give a scor-
pion? If you then, who are evil, know how to give good gifts to
your children, how much more will the heavenly Father give the
Holy Spirit to those who ask him!"*

Guide to the text:
1. Imagine that you have asked Jesus to teach you to pray.
   Read the text as his personal response to you.
2. Pray each phrase of the Lord's prayer. Pause. Reflect on
   how it connects with your life.
3. Pray this model prayer in its entirety without permitting
   your mind to wander. Each time your attention is interrupted, begin the prayer again.
4. Write your reflections on this prayer, indicating how it
   connects with your life at this time.

Alternative guide to the text:
*Pray Psalm 130 a phrase at a time. Think deeply about the
meaning of this prayer for your own life.*

*During the day repeat this prayer: "Lord Jesus, Son of God,
have mercy on me, a sinner." Repeat it during every waking*

hour. Note in your journal your experience with this form of prayer.

Lord Jesus, as I seek to obey the call you are extending to me, teach me to do all things in the Spirit and in the power of prayer.

FIFTEENTH DIRECTIVE

Receive Your Healing

Christ has both the intention and the power to heal us of all infirmities that hinder our obedience. Persons in need of healing must become aware of their needs, come to Christ, and confess their desires to him. Sometimes the healing of Christ occurs in an instant, "in the twinkling of an eye," but at other times the healing takes time. To some Christ speaks healing without hesitation but others must wait patiently for him to work out his will. Still others must await the resurrection. However he heals, Christ wills all persons to be made whole.

Psalm 103:1–5: *Bless the LORD, O my soul, and all that is within me, bless his holy name. Bless the LORD, O my soul, and do not forget all his benefits—who forgives all your iniquity, who heals all your diseases, who redeems your life from the Pit, who crowns you with steadfast love and mercy, who satisfies you with good as long as you live so that your youth is renewed like the eagle's.*

O Christ, your call both overwhelms me with the generosity of your love and frightens me with its consuming demands. I am corrupted by pride, which prevents your holy will. "Good Lord, deliver me."

Text: Mark 1:40–45 *A leper came to him begging him, and kneeling he said to him, "If you choose, you can make me clean." Moved with pity, Jesus stretched out his hand and touched him, and said to him, "I do choose. Be made clean!" Immediately the leprosy left him, and he was made clean. After sternly warning him he sent him away at once, saying to him, "See that you say*

*nothing to anyone; but go, show yourself to the priest, and offer
for your cleansing what Moses commanded, as a testimony to
them." But he went out and began to proclaim it freely, and to
spread the word, so that Jesus could no longer go into a town
openly, but stayed out in the country; and people came to him
from every quarter.*

Guide to the text:
1. Think of yourself as the leper. (Whatever obstructs the
   way of Christ in your life is leprosy.)
2. Imagine yourself coming to Jesus asking for help. Picture
   the time, place, atmosphere, your feelings of helplessness,
   your desires, and so forth.
3. Write a first-person account of how you decided to go to
   Jesus; what it was like making the trip. Describe the
   thoughts in your mind and the feelings that you experienced when you came to Jesus.
4. When Jesus has healed you, remain in his presence and
   ask him the question that comes most readily to your
   mind. Write his response. Continue to write a dialogue
   with him as long as any thoughts come to you.
5. Spend time in silence with the ideas that emerged in your
   writing.

Alternative guide to the text:
*Stand naked before a full-length mirror. Look at your body.
Focus on your eyes and look yourself squarely in the eye. Ask yourself, "What is the leprosy in my life? What makes me unaccept-
able? Unapproachable?" Record the insights that come to you.*

Lord Jesus, touch me. Make me whole. May your mighty
power purge me of all that hinders the fulfillment of your perfect will in me.

SIXTEENTH DIRECTIVE

Follow Your Call into the Kingdom of God

God invites each of us into a personal relationship with Christ. In this relationship we learn the meaning of our lives and the pathways we are to take. This call of God is personal but not private; God calls us to a relationship much greater, to become a citizen of the Kingdom of Heaven. The kingdom embraces the whole world; as a movement it enlists persons, calls forth compassion, seeks peace among all peoples, and demands justice for the poor and powerless. God's purpose in history will be realized only when all persons participate fully as citizens in the kingdom.

Psalm 24:3–10: *Who shall ascend the hill of the LORD? And who shall stand in his holy place? Those who have clean hands and pure hearts, who do not lift up their souls to what is false, and do not swear deceitfully. They will receive blessing from the LORD, and vindication from the God of their salvation. Such is the company of those who seek him, who seek the face of the God of Jacob. Lift up your heads, O gates! and be lifted up, O ancient doors! that the King of glory may come in. Who is the King of glory? The LORD, strong and mighty, the LORD, mighty in battle. Lift up your heads, O gates! and be lifted up, O ancient doors! that the King of glory may come in. Who is this King of glory? The LORD of hosts, he is the King of glory.*

Lord Jesus, you have planted the seed of the kingdom in my heart. Make the soil of my soul good and grant me the courage to choose your divine purpose over every competing loyalty.

Text: Matthew 13:1–9 *That same day Jesus went out of the house and sat beside the sea. Such great crowds gathered around him that he got into a boat and sat there, while the whole crowd stood on the beach. And he told them many things in parables, saying: "Listen! A sower went out to sow. And as he sowed, some seeds fell on the path, and the birds came and ate them up. Other seeds fell on rocky ground, where they did not have much soil, and they sprang up quickly, since they had no depth of soil. But when the sun rose, they were scorched; and since they had no root, they withered away. Other seeds fell among thorns, and the thorns grew up and choked them. Other seeds fell on good soil and brought forth grain, some a hundredfold, some sixty, some thirty. Let anyone with ears listen!" Then the disciples came and asked him, "Why do you speak to them in parables?" He answered, "To you it has been given to know the secrets of the Kingdom of Heaven, but to them it has not been given."*

Guide to the text:
1. Imagine that each kind of soil depicts a different type of human consciousness. Which seems to represent your own consciousness?
2. Paraphrase this relationship in a personal way by completing this sentence: "My heart is like… soil when I…
3. Imagine the result of your call as it matures in this type of soil (human consciousness).
4. Face squarely the cost of clearing and cultivating the soil of your life to make it good soil for maturing the call of Christ.
5. Let the discoveries in this passage become the substance of your prayer. Write the prayer that flows from your convictions.

Alternative guide to the text:
Choose four bowls. Fill one with rocks, another with hard clay, another with soil in which grass is growing, and a fourth with

potting soil. Spend time contemplating these four samples of soil for a week. Write your reflections.

Or, write an essay describing how each of the four soils is part of your life and how each affects your call.

Lord Jesus, grant me both the courage and the strength to exclude everything that will hinder a perfect obedience to your holy will. Make me a faithful citizen of your kingdom in fulfilling your call.

SEVENTEENTH DIRECTIVE

Give Yourself to Serve

Jesus, the Son of God, came among us as a servant. He made the needs of others his agenda. Forgetting his own comfort and pleasure, he fed the hungry, healed the sick, and encouraged the fainthearted. To follow Christ into the Kingdom of God we must take the towel and basin and wash others' feet. The call to follow is foremost a call to serve.

Psalm 86:1–11: *Incline your ear, O LORD, and answer me, for I am poor and needy. Preserve my life, for I am devoted to you; save your servant who trusts in you. You are my God; be gracious to me, O LORD, for to you do I cry all day long. Gladden the soul of your servant, for to you, O LORD, I lift up my soul. For you, O LORD, are good and forgiving, abounding in steadfast love to all who call on you. Give ear, O LORD, to my prayer; listen to my cry of supplication. In the day of my trouble I call on you, for you will answer me. There is none like you among the gods, O LORD, nor are there any works like yours. All the nations you have made shall come and bow down before you, O LORD, and shall glorify your name. For you are great and do wondrous things; you alone are God. Teach me your way, O LORD, that I may walk in your truth; give me an undivided heart to revere your name.*

Lord Jesus, help me to receive your call to serve with humility and fulfill it faithfully.

Text: John 13:1–17 *Now before the festival of the Passover, Jesus knew that his hour had come to depart from this world and go to the Father. Having loved his own who were in the world, he* *loved them to the end. The devil had already put it into the heart of Judas son of Simon Iscariot to betray him. And during supper Jesus, knowing that the Father had given all things into his hands, and that he had come from God and was going to God, got up from the table, took off his outer robe, and tied a towel around himself. Then he poured water into a basin and began to wash the disciples' feet and to wipe them with the towel that was tied around him. He came to Simon Peter, who said to him, "Lord, are you going to wash my feet?" Jesus answered, "You do not know now what I am doing, but later you will understand." Peter said to him, "You will never wash my feet." Jesus answered, "Unless I wash you, you have no share with me." Simon Peter said to him, "Lord, not my feet only but also my hands and my head!" Jesus said to him, "One who has bathed does not need to wash, except for the feet, but is entirely clean. And you are clean, though not all of you." For he knew who was to betray him; for this reason he said, "Not all of you are clean."*

After he had washed their feet, had put on his robe, and had returned to the table, he said to them, "Do you know what I have done to you? You call me Teacher and Lord—and you are right, for that is what I am. So if I, your Lord and Teacher, have washed your feet, you also ought to wash one another's feet. For I have set you an example, that you also should do as I have done to you. Very truly, I tell you, servants are not greater than their master, nor are messengers greater than the one who sent them. If you know these things, you are blessed if you do them."

Guide to the text:

1. Read the account of Jesus washing the disciples' feet and note the various movements of Jesus (rose from supper, laid aside his garments, etc.).
2. Prepare yourself to meditate on this encounter. Literally take off your shoes and socks or hose in preparation for

this experience. (See the Introduction for help with meditation.)

3.   Place yourself in the circle of disciples. Picture Jesus, washing each disciple's feet. Imagine what he says to each.

4.   When he comes to you, look into his eyes, see his hands, feel his touch, experience his hands washing your feet. Sit for a while, watching him kneel before you. Let yourself become fully aware of who he is and what he is doing to you.

5.   Write a dialogue with Jesus that begins with the words, "Lord when you wash my feet, I feel..."

Alternative guide to the text:

In the servant spirit of Jesus, today do one, kind, unselfish act of service without calling attention to your act or without expecting any reward. Write a reflection on the act.

Lord Jesus, as you have loved me and served me, give me grace to love and serve others with the same spirit.

EIGHTEENTH DIRECTIVE

Partake of His Body and His Blood

To eat the bread and drink the wine of the sacrament is to partake of Christ; to partake of his Spirit empowers us to do what he did, to suffer what he suffered, and to be faithful as he was. Each time we take the bread or drink the cup we proclaim to the world that he has come, is coming, and will come at the end of the age! No other act so greatly empowers our call.

Psalm 39:4–6: *LORD, let me know my end, and what is the measure of my days; let me know how fleeting my life is. You have made my days a few handbreadths, and my lifetime is as nothing in your sight. Surely everyone stands as a mere breath. Surely everyone goes about like a shadow. Surely for nothing they are in turmoil; they heap up, and do not know who will gather.*

Lord Jesus, as I obey your call, reveal to me the mystery of your body and blood forgiving my sins, reminding me of you and empowering my life.

Text: Matthew 26:17–39 *On the first day of Unleavened Bread the disciples came to Jesus, saying, "Where do you want us to make the preparations for you to eat the Passover?" He said, "Go into the city to a certain man, and say to him, 'The Teacher says, My time is near; I will keep the Passover at your house with my disciples.'" So the disciples did as Jesus had directed them, and they prepared the Passover meal.*

When it was evening, he took his place with the twelve; and while they were eating, he said, "Truly I tell you, one of you will betray me." And they became greatly distressed and began to say to him one after another, "Surely not I, Lord?" He answered,

"The one who has dipped his hand into the bowl with me will betray me. The Son of Man goes as it is written of him, but woe to that one by whom the Son of Man is betrayed! It would have been better for that one not to have been born." Judas, who betrayed him, said, "Surely not I, Rabbi?" He replied, "You have said so." While they were eating, Jesus took a loaf of bread, and after blessing it he broke it, gave it to the disciples, and said, "Take, eat; this is my body." Then he took a cup, and after giving thanks he gave it to them, saying, "Drink from it, all of you; for this is my blood of the covenant, which is poured out for many for the forgiveness of sins. I tell you, I will never again drink of this fruit of the vine until that day when I drink it new with you in my Father's kingdom." When they had sung the hymn, they went out to the Mount of Olives. Then Jesus said to them, "You will all become deserters because of me this night; for it is written, 'I will strike the shepherd, and the sheep of the flock will be scattered.' But after I am raised up, I will go ahead of you to Galilee." Peter said to him, "Though all become deserters because of you, I will never desert you." Jesus said to him, "Truly I tell you, this very night, before the cock crows, you will deny me three times." Peter said to him, "Even though I must die with you, I will not deny you." And so said all the disciples.

Guide to the text:

1. Prepare yourself to meditate on the scripture.
2. Picture in your mind the setting for the Lord's last supper: room, table, guests, light, sounds, feeling you have, food on the table—everything.
3. See in your mind each disciple receiving the bread and wine. Repeat his words: "This is my body…this is my blood." As you sit at the table, hear him speak these words to you. (Being present to him, listening to his words, and feeling the result are important.)
4. After you leave the Upper Room, write a first-person

account of your experience at the supper. Be sure to include the use of all your senses.

Alternative guide to the text:
After meditating on the text, pour a glass of wine, break a piece of bread, and lay the broken bread on a plate. Sit before this bread and this wine for fifteen minutes thinking about what it means for you.

Lord Jesus, let this bread and wine become symbols of your life in me and of my communion with you.

NINETEENTH DIRECTIVE

Face Betrayal by a Friend

Those committed to do the will of God often face disappointment with the persons who claim to be their friends. No pain cuts deeper than the pain of betrayal by a friend. We cannot control the failure of brothers and sisters with its consequent pain, but we can choose our responses to them and we can find healing for our own pain. Knowing the hurt caused by unfaithfulness, let us not add to Christ's pain with our betrayal. The virtue of loyalty surpasses all our promises of love and good intentions.

Psalm 55:1, 12–14, 20–21: *Give ear to my prayer, O God; do not hide yourself from my supplication… It is not enemies who taunt me—I could bear that; it is not adversaries who deal insolently with me—I could hide from them. But it is you, my equal, my companion, my familiar friend, with whom I kept pleasant company; we walked in the house of God with the throng… My companion laid hands on a friend and violated a covenant with me with speech smoother than butter, but with a heart set on war; with words that were softer than oil, but in fact were drawn swords.*

Lord Jesus Christ, grant that I may see with my eyes and feel with my heart the pain you experienced in the betrayal by a friend so that as your friend I will never betray you.

Text: Matthew 26:14–16, 20–25, 47–50 *Then one of the twelve, who was called Judas Iscariot, went to the chief priests and said, "What will you give me if I betray him to you?" They paid him thirty pieces of silver. And from that moment he began*

to look for an opportunity to betray him....When it was evening,
he took his place with the twelve; and while they were eating, he
said, "Truly I tell you, one of you will betray me."

And they became greatly distressed and began to say to him
one after another, "Surely not I, Lord?" He answered, "The one
who has dipped his hand into the bowl with me will betray me.
The Son of Man goes as it is written of him, but woe to that one
by whom the Son of Man is betrayed! It would have been better
for that one not to have been born." Judas, who betrayed him,
said, "Surely not I, Rabbi?" He replied, "You have said so."...

[Later, in Gethsemane] Judas, one of the twelve, arrived;
with him was a large crowd with swords and clubs, from the
chief priests and the elders of the people.

Now the betrayer had given them a sign, saying, "The one I
will kiss is the man; arrest him." At once he came up to Jesus and
said, "Greetings, Rabbi!" and kissed him.

Jesus said to him, "Friend, do what you are here to do." Then
they came and laid hands on Jesus and arrested him.

Guide to the text:

1. Replay in your mind the events leading to Christ's arrest; let the backs of your eyelids become television screens for the viewing.
2. Write a first-person confession by Judas. Be sure to include Judas's motives and feelings, the consequences, and his personal outcome. Begin the confession with the words "My name is Judas Iscariot and I betrayed Jesus of Nazareth."
3. As you look honestly into your own heart, what do you see that would lead you to betray the Lord's call to you?

Alternative guide to the text:

Think of a friend that you have betrayed through ignorance,
neglect, or sheer thoughtlessness. Ask him or her to forgive you.

What do you think would have happened to Judas if he had asked forgiveness?

Lord Jesus, when I would choose the easy way, the selfish way, or the rebellious way, remind me of the pain this causes you as well as those who trust me.

TWENTIETH DIRECTIVE

Pray the Only Prayer

God has created the world for a purpose. In the divine economy, human beings made in the image of God uniquely participate in the fulfillment of that divine intention. In all the vicissitudes of life the only worthy goal is the will of God, done on earth as it is in heaven. In the pursuit of the divine intention for our lives there is finally but one prayer to pray: "Thy will be done, thy kingdom come."

Psalm 103:17–22: *But the steadfast love of the LORD is from everlasting to everlasting on those who fear him, and his righteousness to children's children, to those who keep his covenant and remember to do his commandments. The LORD has established his throne in the heavens, and his kingdom rules over all. Bless the LORD, O you his angels, you mighty ones who do his bidding, obedient to his spoken word. Bless the LORD, all his hosts, his ministers that do his will. Bless the LORD, all his works, in all places of his dominion. Bless the LORD, O my soul.*

Lord Jesus, in every struggle that I face grant me a single-minded prayer of ultimate surrender: "Your will, not mine be done."

Text: Matthew 26:36–46 *Then Jesus went with them to a place called Gethsemane; and he said to his disciples, "Sit here while I go over there and pray." He took with him Peter and the two sons of Zebedee, and began to be grieved and agitated. Then he said to them, "I am deeply grieved, even to death; remain here, and stay awake with me." And going a little farther, he threw himself on the ground and prayed, "My Father, if it is possible, let*

this cup pass from me; yet not what I want but what you want."
Then he came to the disciples and found them sleeping; and he
said to Peter, "So, could you not stay awake with me one hour?
Stay awake and pray that you may not come into the time of
trial; the spirit indeed is willing, but the flesh is weak." Again he
went away for the second time and prayed, "My Father, if this
cannot pass unless I drink it, your will be done." Again he came
and found them sleeping, for their eyes were heavy. So leaving
them again, he went away and prayed for the third time, saying
the same words. Then he came to the disciples and said to them,
"Are you still sleeping and taking your rest? See, the hour is at
hand, and the Son of Man is betrayed into the hands of sinners.
Get up, let us be going. See, my betrayer is at hand."

Guide to the text:

1. Prepare yourself to engage the text.
2. Imagine the details of the setting: trees, bushes, rocks, the cold earth, darkness of the night, the heavy atmosphere, clouds covering the moon, the drowsiness of the disciples, and the crisis for Jesus.
3. Consider Jesus' struggle: You have been sent by God to fulfill a unique role in human history and your obedience to God has brought you to the verge of death. Repeat the garden prayer as Jesus might have prayed it. (Say it several times, noticing your associations with the prayer.)
4. When you have completed the meditation as suggested in steps 2 and 3, write a first-person account of what it was like for you to participate in the garden experience with Jesus.

Alternative guide to the text:

Identify one person in your life with whom you have stubbornly demanded your way, go to this person and surrender to him or her. If we cannot surrender to a fellow human being, can we really surrender to God? Jesus did both!

And now, O Righteous Father, what shall I pray? "Save me from this hour?" No! It was for this hour I have come into the world. Father, glorify yourself with the glory we shared before the world began.

TWENTY-FIRST DIRECTIVE

The Denial

Loyalty to Christ demonstrates faithfulness that originates with choosing the will of God over our own will. The sacrifice of oneself for the sake of Christ does not come naturally or easily. Because of limited perception, true believers struggle to know God's will and then their imperfect wills often fail to obey the divine intention even when it is known. Both the lure of pleasure and occasional threats to life and limb present temptations to betray our call and deny our Lord.

Psalm 39:1–5: *I said, "I will guard my ways that I may not sin with my tongue; I will keep a muzzle on my mouth as long as the wicked are in my presence." I was silent and still; I held my peace to no avail; my distress grew worse, my heart became hot within me. While I mused, the fire burned; then I spoke with my tongue: "LORD, let me know my end, and what is the measure of my days; let me know how fleeting my life is. You have made my days a few handbreadths, and my lifetime is as nothing in your sight. Surely everyone stands as a mere breath."*
Gracious Lord, who knows all things, you know that I wish to be faithful to you. Show to me what is in my heart that would cause me to deny you.

Text: Matthew 26:31–35, 57–58, 69–75 *Then Jesus said to them, "You will all become deserters because of me this night; for it is written, 'I will strike the shepherd, and the sheep of the flock will be scattered.' But after I am raised up, I will go ahead of you to Galilee." Peter said to him, "Though all become deserters because of you, I will never desert you." Jesus said to him, "Truly*

66

I tell you, this very night, before the cock crows, you will deny me three times." Peter said to him, "Even though I must die with you, I will not deny you." And so said all the disciples....

Those who had arrested Jesus took him to Caiaphas the high priest, in whose house the scribes and the elders had gathered. But Peter was following him at a distance, as far as the court-yard of the high priest; and going inside, he sat with the guards in order to see how this would end....

Now Peter was sitting outside in the courtyard. A servant-girl came to him and said, "You also were with Jesus the Galilean." But he denied it before all of them, saying, "I do not know what you are talking about." When he went out to the porch, another servant-girl saw him, and she said to the bystanders, "This man was with Jesus of Nazareth." Again he denied it with an oath, "I do not know the man." After a little while the bystanders came up and said to Peter, "Certainly you are also one of them, for your accent betrays you." Then he began to curse, and he swore an oath, "I do not know the man!" At that moment the cock crowed. Then Peter remembered what Jesus had said: "Before the cock crows, you will deny me three times." And he went out and wept bitterly.

Guide to the text:

1. Reread the text and get clearly in mind the sequence of events. Close your eyes and picture the events without words, as if viewing a television program with the sound turned off.

2. Write a loyalty pledge Peter might have constructed on the night of the Passover when he said, "Even though I die with you, I will never deny you."

3. Free-associate with the events of the denial. How do these events connect with your life? What memories come to your mind? What temptations to doubt, disobey, or deny your call do you think of?

4. In your quiet before Christ, confess your denials. Open
    the wounds for healing and release.

Alternative guide to the text:
*Think back over your life for the last week. Identify the times
that voluntarily or by neglect you denied your identity as a
Christian. In your reflection, affirm your true identity as a follower of Christ in one of those situations.*

My Lord and my God, I give thanks to you for revealing to
me how prone I am to deny you and seek my own will. But
you have been quick to offer your grace and to show mercy
undeserved.

TWENTY-SECOND DIRECTIVE

Contemplate His Death

The one who completely understood and perfectly performed the will of God was crucified as a common criminal. Jesus demonstrated fidelity to the will of God under the most severe stress a human can experience. He expressed the depth of the love of God for sinful, broken humanity. Because he has endured the worst in human rejection and pain, he can give comfort and healing to all those who suffer injustice and pain in their efforts to live out a costly obedience.

Psalm 22:9–18: *Yet it was you who took me from the womb; you kept me safe on my mother's breast. On you I was cast from my birth, and since my mother bore me you have been my God. Do not be far from me, for trouble is near and there is no one to help. Many bulls encircle me, strong bulls of Bashan surround me; they open wide their mouths at me, like a ravening and roaring lion. I am poured out like water, and all my bones are out of joint; my heart is like wax; it is melted within my breast; my mouth is dried up like a potsherd, and my tongue sticks to my jaws; you lay me in the dust of death. For dogs are all around me; a company of evildoers encircles me. My hands and feet have shriveled; I can count all my bones. They stare and gloat over me; they divide my clothes among themselves, and for my clothing they cast lots.*

Lord God, make me understand that obedience to your will does not exempt me from suffering and sometimes leads to death.

Text: Matthew 27:1–2, 11–13, 24–26, 45–50, 54. *When morning came, all the chief priests and the elders of the people* *conferred together against Jesus in order to bring about his death. They bound him, led him away, and handed him over to Pilate the governor....*

Now Jesus stood before the governor; and the governor asked him, "Are you the King of the Jews?" Jesus said, "You say so." But when he was accused by the chief priests and elders, he did not answer. Then Pilate said to him, "Do you not hear how many accusations they make against you?"...

So when Pilate saw that he could do nothing, but rather that a riot was beginning, he took some water and washed his hands before the crowd, saying, "I am innocent of this man's blood; see to it yourselves." Then the people as a whole answered, "His blood be on us and on our children!" So he released Barabbas for them; and after flogging Jesus, he handed him over to be crucified....

From noon on, darkness came over the whole land until three in the afternoon.

And about three o'clock Jesus cried with a loud voice, "Eli, Eli, lema sabachthani?" that is, "My God, my God, why have you forsaken me?" When some of the bystanders heard it, they said, "This man is calling for Elijah." At once one of them ran and got a sponge, filled it with sour wine, put it on a stick, and gave it to him to drink. But the others said, "Wait, let us see whether Elijah will come to save him." Then Jesus cried again with a loud voice and breathed his last....

Now when the centurion and those with him, who were keeping watch over Jesus, saw the earthquake and what took place, they were terrified and said, "Truly this man was God's Son!"

Guide to the text:
1. In your imagination, walk the Via de la Rosa with Jesus to the cross. What sounds do you hear? What do you see? What are the feelings you have?
2. Imagine that Jesus looked at you from the cross and

began speaking to you. Write a long paragraph of what you think he says to you.
3. In your mind withdraw from the cross and find a quiet place to think about what he has said. Record the feelings that you have about his words to you.
4. Ponder the question: "For what am I willing to die?"

Alternative guide to the text:
Find a dark, cave-like place in your home (a closet, a bathroom without a window, etc.) and lie down with the doors closed. Think of this small space with its darkness as representing the tomb in which you have been laid with Jesus. Remain in a prone position in this place for twenty minutes. Later, in your journal reflect on what it is like to be joined to Christ in his death.

Lord, grant me the courage to accept accusations and rebuffs in silence and to yield myself to die if obedience to you requires it.

TWENTY-THIRD DIRECTIVE

Share in His Resurrection

The Lord who became flesh suffered, died, and was buried, and on the third day he arose and lives forever. As believers we participate in Jesus' death and in his resurrection. Death that threatens hope has been overcome; we are freed from its power to live abundantly and even to sacrifice our lives for his sake. Through baptism we share in the Eternal Purpose of God, now and forever! The fulfillment of our calling constitutes a fragment of the cosmic enterprise of God.

Psalm 16:7–11: *I bless the LORD who gives me counsel; in the night also my heart instructs me. I keep the LORD always before me; because he is at my right hand, I shall not be moved. Therefore my heart is glad, and my soul rejoices; my body also rests secure. For you do not give me up to Sheol, or let your faithful one see the Pit. You show me the path of life. In your presence there is fullness of joy; in your right hand are pleasures forevermore.*

Risen Christ, help me to see in your death and resurrection the foundation and power of my call to participate in your kingdom.

Text: Luke 23:50–56; 24:1–12, 36–49 *Now there was a good and righteous man named Joseph, who, though a member of the council, had not agreed to their plan and action. He came from the Jewish town of Arimathea, and he was waiting expectantly for the kingdom of God. This man went to Pilate and asked for the body of Jesus. Then he took it down, wrapped it in a* *linen cloth, and laid it in a rock-hewn tomb where no one had ever been laid. It was the day of Preparation, and the sabbath was beginning. The women who had come with him from Galilee followed, and they saw the tomb and how his body was laid. Then they returned, and prepared spices and ointments. On the sabbath they rested according to the commandment.*

But on the first day of the week, at early dawn, they came to the tomb, taking the spices that they had prepared. They found the stone rolled away from the tomb, but when they went in, they did not find the body. While they were perplexed about this, suddenly two men in dazzling clothes stood beside them. The women were terrified and bowed their faces to the ground, but the men said to them, "Why do you look for the living among the dead? He is not here, but has risen. Remember how he told you, while he was still in Galilee, that the Son of Man must be handed over to sinners, and be crucified, and on the third day rise again." Then they remembered his words, and returning from the tomb, they told all this to the eleven and to all the rest. Now it was Mary Magdalene, Joanna, Mary the mother of James, and the other women with them who told this to the apostles. But these words seemed to them an idle tale, and they did not believe them. But Peter got up and ran to the tomb; stooping and looking in, he saw the linen cloths by themselves; then he went home, amazed at what had happened....

While they were talking about this, Jesus himself stood among them and said to them, "Peace be with you." They were startled and terrified, and thought that they were seeing a ghost. He said to them, "Why are you frightened, and why do doubts arise in your hearts? Look at my hands and my feet; see that it is I myself. Touch me and see; for a ghost does not have flesh and bones as you see that I have." And when he had said this, he showed them his hands and his feet. While in their joy they were disbelieving and still wondering, he said to them, "Have you anything here to

*eat?" They gave him a piece of broiled fish, and he took it and
ate in their presence.*

*Then he said to them, "These are my words that I spoke to you
while I was still with you—that everything written about me in
the law of Moses, the prophets, and the psalms must be fulfilled."
Then he opened their minds to understand the scriptures, and he
said to them, "Thus it is written, that the Messiah is to suffer
and to rise from the dead on the third day, and that repentance
and forgiveness of sins is to be proclaimed in his name to all
nations, beginning from Jerusalem. You are witnesses of these
things. And see, I am sending upon you what my Father
promised; so stay here in the city until you have been clothed with
power from on high."*

Guide to the text:

1. Spend time meditating on these three episodes—the burial, resurrection, and the commissioning.
   - The burial. Experience the burial of Jesus with each of the five senses—sight, sound, smell, touch, and taste. If you are a woman at the tomb, what are you thinking?
   - The resurrection. Imaginatively, identify with the women who are taking spices to the tomb on the first day of the week. What are they feeling on the way? What are they discussing? When they see the empty tomb, what do they feel?
   - The appearance. Imagine you are seated at the table with the disciples when Jesus appears. Visualize his presence. Listen to his words. What do you feel?
2. After this meditation on the risen Christ, write a report of your meeting Jesus after his resurrection. "On the first day of the week I met Jesus and…"

Alternative guide to the text:

"See Him Seeing You." It is not so much our seeing him but seeing him seeing us. In your place of prayer get seated comfortably.

Visualize the risen Christ standing behind you, beholding you. For a half hour sit before his risen presence.

Lord Jesus, your mission took you to the cross and to death and yet in total self-surrender you conquered death through the resurrection.

TWENTY-FOURTH DIRECTIVE

Wait for the Promise

The presence of God made manifest in Jesus of Nazareth continues among his people in the Holy Spirit. The Holy Spirit, the presence of Christ with the people and in them, transcends time and space. In the Spirit believers become contemporaneous with the risen Christ. Through the Spirit, Christ comes to them, enters into them and makes his home in them. By the Spirit Christ informs their thoughts and decisions and he acts through them to continue his work in the world. But disciples must wait for the promise of the Spirit to fill them with power, courage, and vision.

Psalm 36:5–9: *Your steadfast love, O LORD, extends to the heavens, your faithfulness to the clouds. Your righteousness is like the mighty mountains, your judgments are like the great deep; you save humans and animals alike, O LORD. How precious is your steadfast love, O God! All people may take refuge in the shadow of your wings. They feast on the abundance of your house, and you give them drink from the river of your delights. For with you is the fountain of life; in your light we see light. Oh, continue your steadfast love to those who know you, and your salvation to the upright of heart!*

Risen Jesus Christ, grant me the courage to believe that you continue to live among us, the faith to receive your presence within myself, and the patience to wait for the coming of the Spirit that you may work through me.

Text: John 14:15–23 *"If you love me, you will keep my commandments. And I will ask the Father, and he will give you another Advocate, to be with you forever. This is the Spirit of truth, whom the world cannot receive, because it neither sees him nor knows him. You know him, because he abides with you, and he will be in you.*

"I will not leave you orphaned; I am coming to you. In a little while the world will no longer see me, but you will see me; because I live, you also will live. On that day you will know that I am in my Father, and you in me, and I in you. They who have my commandments and keep them are those who love me; and those who love me will be loved by my Father, and I will love them and reveal myself to them." Judas (not Iscariot) said to him, "Lord, how is it that you will reveal yourself to us, and not to the world?" Jesus answered him, "Those who love me will keep my word, and my Father will love them, and we will come to them and make our home with them."

Guide to the text:

1. Visualize Jesus with his disciples making the promises contained in these texts.
2. Paraphrase John 14:15–23 and insert yourself and your era into the promises Christ makes regarding the Holy Spirit.
3. Imagine that you are one of the disciples in the Upper Room waiting for the promised Holy Spirit (Acts 1:12–14). Write your thoughts, feelings, fears, and hopes. "Lord Jesus, as I wait for you to come to me in the Spirit…"
4. Make a deliberate act of faith to receive the promised Holy Spirit into your life and consciousness. Expect the presence to evidence itself in "newness."

Alternative guide to the text:

After reading the text carefully and thoughtfully, select three water glasses. Fill one completely full, fill another half full, and

*leave the third empty. Place all three on a table before you in
your place of prayer and look at them; contemplate them for
twenty minutes. Record your thoughts.*

Lord, make me aware of you in me, and in all my life today.

TWENTY-FIFTH DIRECTIVE

Actualize the Mystery of His Body

In the life, death, and resurrection of Jesus of Nazareth, God has reconciled the world. Those who are baptized into him realize their destiny; they are Christ's body on earth. Christ distributes gifts to all the members of his body and he calls each to minister in his name. The Body of Christ receives its fulfillment and it fulfills its mission through the work of the Spirit in each member. Members of the body are signs of his presence, performers of his will, and worshipers of the living God. In community the disciples of Jesus multiply their strength; going it alone they fail.

Psalm 44:1–3: *We have heard with our ears, O God, our ancestors have told us, what deeds you performed in their days, in the days of old: You with your own hand drove out the nations, but them you planted; you afflicted the peoples, but them you set free; for not by their own sword did they win the land, nor did their own arm give them victory; but your right hand, and your arm, and the light of your countenance, for you delighted in them.*

Spirit of God, who creates the Body of Christ on earth and makes me a member of it, show me my place and how my gifts build up the body of our Lord.

Text: Acts 2:1–4 *When the day of Pentecost had come, they were all together in one place. And suddenly from heaven there came a sound like the rush of a violent wind, and it filled the entire house where they were sitting. Divided tongues, as of fire, appeared among them, and a tongue rested on each of them. All* *of them were filled with the Holy Spirit and began to speak in other languages, as the Spirit gave them ability.*

Guide to the text:
1. Meditate on the miracle of Pentecost against the background of the annunciation to Mary that she would conceive in her body the divine presence (Lk 1:26–38). Think of the Spirit—moving upon the womb of the community, creating the corporate Body of Christ, the church.
2. Place yourself in the Upper Room with the disciples waiting for the Spirit to come. What would you be thinking, feeling, wondering, or asking?
3. Imagine the "moment of his coming" when there is suddenly a sound, a wind, a fire, and the Spirit who fills all the members of the Body of Christ. Offer yourself to Christ in your emptiness that he may fill you.
4. Over the next few days notice the people who come into your life, the thoughts that come unbidden, the springs of joy that begin to break loose within you. Let these "happenings" confirm that the Spirit has come and is coming to you!

Alternative guide to the text:
Light a candle and contemplate the fire for half an hour. In your journal, note the ways that this fire symbolizes the Spirit.

Lord, I need help from others for encouragement and support. Help me discern their gifts and have the humility to receive their ministry.

TWENTY-SIXTH DIRECTIVE

Celebrate the Generosity of His Gifts

All followers of Christ have received gifts to enable them to fulfill their call. The Holy Spirit also empowers the members of the Body of Christ to minister in his name. The members depend on each other to identify and affirm their gifts. The use of the gifts builds up the Body of Christ and empowers it for ministry. Gifts empower the body for its ministry both within and beyond the church. Members should do what they are gifted to do, not what others think they ought to do.

Psalm 139:1–6: *O LORD, you have searched me and known me. You know when I sit down and when I rise up; you discern my thoughts from far away. You search out my path and my lying down, and are acquainted with all my ways. Even before a word is on my tongue, O LORD, you know it completely. You hem me in, behind and before, and lay your hand upon me. Such knowledge is too wonderful for me; it is so high that I cannot attain it.*

O Holy Spirit, open my eyes to recognize the gifts which you have given me and make me to understand how to use them to fulfill my calling.

Text: 1 Corinthians 12:1, 4–11 *Now concerning spiritual gifts, brothers and sisters, I do not want you to be uninformed. Now there are varieties of gifts, but the same Spirit; and there are varieties of services, but the same Lord; and there are varieties of activities, but it is the same God who activates all of them in everyone. To each is given the manifestation of the Spirit for the common good. To one is given through the Spirit the utterance of* *wisdom, and to another the utterance of knowledge according to the same Spirit, to another faith by the same Spirit, to another gifts of healing by the one Spirit, to another the working of miracles, to another prophecy, to another the discernment of spirits, to another various kinds of tongues, to another the interpretation of tongues. All these are activated by one and the same Spirit, who allots to each one individually just as the Spirit chooses.*

Guide to the text:
1. Meditate on the gifts listed above. Do you seem to have any of these gifts? Think more deeply about the ones that make you wonder.
2. What are the things that you do easily? To what gifts does this point?
3. What are the things that you most enjoy doing, that bring you the greatest sense of fulfillment? What gifts are required to do these things?
4. What gifts do other spiritually sensitive persons affirm in you? Could this be one way to discern your gifts?
5. What do you have a passion to do?
6. After brooding over these questions that point toward your gifts, make a list of the gifts that you believe you have. Find a friend and share your lists of gifts and request your friend's correction or confirmation.

Alternative guide to the text:
Make a list, in three columns, of things (1) you do well; (2) you enjoy doing; (3) you have a passion for doing. What gifts are required to do these things?

Lord Jesus, I pray for a deeper understanding of your gifts to me and a greater trust in your willingness to express yourself through me.

TWENTY-SEVENTH DIRECTIVE

Be a Good Steward of the Mystery

Each member of the body has been called to minister in the Spirit of Christ and has been granted gifts for the task. Gifts for ministry are not personal possessions of the member; they are grants, bequests, or pledges to be used to build up the whole Body of Christ to the glory of God. A steward cares for the goods and responds to the desires of another. Christians are stewards of a call, a gift(s), and a ministry and to these we must be faithful.

Psalm 63:1–4: *O God, you are my God, I seek you, my soul thirsts for you; my flesh faints for you, as in a dry and weary land where there is no water. So I have looked upon you in the sanctuary, beholding your power and glory. Because your steadfast love is better than life, my lips will praise you. So I will bless you as long as I live; I will lift up my hands and call on your name. My soul is satisfied as with a rich feast, and my mouth praises you with joyful lips when I think of you on my bed, and meditate on you in the watches of the night; for you have been my help, and in the shadow of your wings I sing for joy.*

Spirit of the Living Christ, grant to me strength of will and constancy of faith that I may be a trustworthy servant of your kingdom.

Text: 1 Corinthians 4:1–7 *Think of us in this way, as servants of Christ and stewards of God's mysteries. Moreover, it is required of stewards that they be found trustworthy. But with me it is a very small thing that I should be judged by you or by any human court. I do not even judge myself. I am not aware of*

83

anything against myself, but I am not hereby acquitted. It is the Lord who judges me. Therefore do not pronounce judgment before the time, before the Lord comes, who will bring to light the things now hidden in darkness and will disclose the purposes of the heart. Then each one will receive commendation from God. I have applied all this to Apollos and myself for your benefit, brothers and sisters, so that you may learn through us the meaning of the saying, "Nothing beyond what is written," so that none of you will be puffed up in favor of one against another. For who sees anything different in you? What do you have that you did not receive? And if you received it, why do you boast as if it were not a gift?

Guide to the text:

1. Meditate on this text, paying special attention to the three questions at the end. Answer these candidly.
2. Write a scenario describing where you think that your call is leading you and how it will finally come out. Perhaps it would be interesting to write this in the third person.

Alternative guide to the text:

Christian mystic Julian of Norwich says that one of the joys of heaven will be that our Lord will personally thank us for the work we have done in his name and he will tell others what we have done. What do you think he will thank you for and what will he say to others about you?

Lord Jesus, grant me the grace to be faithful to your call so that all you have intended through my life may be accomplished.

TWENTY-EIGHTH DIRECTIVE

Live Worthy of Your Call

The person called by Christ gives the most convincing testimony to faith by demonstrating neighbor-love. In part, the authority for ministry emerges out of the integrity of our lives. A profession of devotion without the performance of love and humility creates doubt and confusion both in the follower of Christ and in the Christian community. Faithful obedience expressed in gracious love creates an enduring symbol of our Lord Jesus Christ.

Psalm 131: *O LORD, my heart is not lifted up, my eyes are not raised too high; I do not occupy myself with things too great and too marvelous for me. But I have calmed and quieted my soul, like a weaned child with its mother; my soul is like the weaned child that is with me. O Israel, hope in the LORD from this time on and forevermore.*

Spirit of Christ, reveal within me the Spirit of Jesus who forgave the undeserving, healed the broken-hearted, sought the lowest place of service, and sacrificed himself in love.

Text: John 8:2–11 *Early in the morning he came again to the temple. All the people came to him and he sat down and began to teach them. The scribes and the Pharisees brought a woman who had been caught in adultery; and making her stand before all of them, they said to him, "Teacher, this woman was caught in the very act of committing adultery. Now in the law Moses commanded us to stone such women. Now what do you say?" They said this to test him, so that they might have some charge to bring against him. Jesus bent down and wrote with his* *finger on the ground. When they kept on questioning him, he straightened up and said to them, "Let anyone among you who is without sin be the first to throw a stone at her."*

And once again he bent down and wrote on the ground.

When they heard it, they went away, one by one, beginning with the elders; and Jesus was left alone with the woman standing before him. Jesus straightened up and said to her, "Woman, where are they? Has no one condemned you?"

She said, "No one, sir." And Jesus said, "Neither do I condemn you. Go your way, and from now on do not sin again."

Guide to the text:

1. In this story we meet the victim, the persecutors, and the liberator. Review the story three times from each of these perspectives.
2. Identify traces of each of these three persons in your own life.
3. How does Jesus resolve the conflict between faithfulness and grace?
4. What do you learn from Jesus about faithfulness?

Alternative guide to the text:

Think of someone in your life who is being victimized. Seek out that person and offer acceptance and freedom. Write your reflections in your journal.

Lord Jesus, cleanse my heart and life of all unloving memories, attitudes, and actions so that I may free others who are oppressed with guilt and failure.

TWENTY-NINTH DIRECTIVE

Receive the Promise of Presence

Obedient disciples are not alone on the journey of kingdom service. Christ is with them; Christ is in them. Christ promised to come again. Ten days after his departure he came in the power of the Spirit, filling the lives of his followers with a consciousness of his presence. Through this divine presence the disciples of Jesus received the power to obey their Lord and to do his will. That same Holy Spirit is promised to each of us.

Psalm 107:1–9: *Oh, give thanks to the LORD, for he is good; for his steadfast love endures forever. Let the redeemed of the LORD say so, those he redeemed from trouble and gathered in from the lands, from the east and from the west, from the north and from the south. Some wandered in desert wastes, finding no way to an inhabited town; hungry and thirsty, their soul fainted within them. Then they cried to the LORD in their trouble, and he delivered them from their distress; he led them by a straight way, until they reached an inhabited town. Let them thank the LORD for his steadfast love, for his wonderful works to humankind. For he satisfies the thirsty, and the hungry he fills with good things.*

O Holy Spirit, prepare me in mind and heart to receive your living presence that I may indeed become a person in whom the Spirit lives.

Text: John 14:15–25 *"If you love me, you will keep my commandments. And I will ask the Father, and he will give you another Advocate, to be with you forever. This is the Spirit of truth, whom the world cannot receive, because it neither sees him nor knows him. You know him, because he abides with you, and he will* *be in you. I will not leave you orphaned; I am coming to you. In a little while the world will no longer see me, but you will see me; because I live, you also will live. On that day you will know that I am in my Father, and you in me, and I in you. They who have my commandments and keep them are those who love me; and those who love me will be loved by my Father, and I will love them and reveal myself to them." Judas (not Iscariot) said to him, "Lord, how is it that you will reveal yourself to us, and not to the world?" Jesus answered him, "Those who love me will keep my word, and my Father will love them, and we will come to them and make our home with them. Whoever does not love me does not keep my words; and the word that you hear is not mine, but is from the Father who sent me. I have said these things to you while I am still with you...."*

Guide to the text:

1. Read the text as though you are sitting in the circle with the disciples. Jesus focuses his attention on you and speaks the words of the text to you as if you were the only person present. Record your thoughts, your feelings, and the images that his address inspires in you.

2. Review the events of your life yesterday. What evidence of the presence of Christ do you note? What could have occurred because of him? Write down possibilities.

3. Write a prayer requesting the divine presence to permeate your life.

Alternative guide to the text:

Meditate on this text until you can visualize the presence of Christ and the Father through the Spirit abiding in you. Draw a picture with pen or crayon that symbolizes this reality.

Lord Jesus Christ, in company with the Father and the blessed Holy Spirit, you have promised to live in and through me. Grant me a pure obedience to prepare my heart and a deeply sensitive spirit to recognize your presence.

THIRTIETH DIRECTIVE

Read your statement from the Second Directive describing your need for discernment in your life.

Review each of the directives and summarize your discoveries in a short essay of two or three pages.

An alternative suggestion:

Review your issue of discernment. Review your insights from each of the directives and summarize them in a one- or two-page essay or in a thoughtful pen or clay rendering. Should you choose to express your learnings in art, be sure to explain them in a supplementary paragraph or two.